Taste Bud Travels

Written by John Parsons

Rigby

Taste Bud Travels

Chapter Snapshots ...

1. Food Origins

Today we can choose from a great variety of food from all around the world. Some foods may not come from where you might think, however!

2. Let's Get Cooking!

Let's take a closer look at how the foods we like to cook often depend on where we live.

"Ever since people have countries, they have beer

3. Don't Forget To Pack Your Taste Buds!

We wouldn't know about many of our favorite foods if explorers hadn't brought them back from far-away countries for us to try.

4. No Time To Cook?

Sometimes there just isn't enough time to cook, and we need to find food that's fast, tasty, and nutritious!

5. Bon Appetit!

It's common today for people to eat foods from many different cultures. How many foods from different cultures have you tried?

12

been able to travel to different eating new and different foods."

1. Food Origins

If someone asked you where pasta first came from, you might think of spaghetti, lasagna, and ravioli. Your answer might be Italy.

If someone asked you where the potatoes we use for french fries first came from, you might say France.

If someone asked you where the turkeys that we eat at Thanksgiving first came from, you might say Turkey.

These would be good guesses. But they're wrong!

Ever since people have been able to travel to faraway countries, they have been trying unfamiliar foods. Travelers have long brought back foods that they liked to their own countries. Today, many of our favorite foods represent many different cultures around the world.

The Big Turkey Trot

Although turkeys didn't come from Turkey, they traveled a long way before they reached our first Thanksgiving table. Early explorers took tamed turkeys home from Mexico to Europe. Later, pilgrims from Europe brought them back to North America, only to discover that the American woods were full of wild ones!

Before it was possible to store and transport food over long distances, most people could eat only what they could grow or catch in their own part of the world.

That meant that people who didn't live close to rivers, lakes, or an ocean might not eat fish very often. If they lived in a cold part of the world, such as Canada or Norway, they may never have seen or tasted foods grown in hot parts of the world, such as pineapples and mangoes!

People who lived in rainy parts of Asia, where there was plenty of water and mud, would have grown a lot of rice and used that in their cooking. People who lived in Europe or North America, where the climate was drier, would have grown and eaten wheat instead.

The food crops people planted were suited to the environment in which they lived. So were their recipes!

All About Rice

Rice is a type of grass that was first grown in India and Southeast Asia. Rice needs to be grown in fields that are covered in water. Almost one-third of the world's people eat rice as their main food. The part we eat is the kernel of the rice plant.

In some countries, the outer skin, or husk, of the rice kernel is burned to make a special type of ash. When this ash is mixed with other chemicals, it makes cement, which is used to build houses!

"W" Is For Wheat

Wheat is a type of grass. It was originally grown in the Middle East. Wheat grows best in climates that are not too hot or too cold. The main suppliers of wheat are Australia, Canada, some parts of Europe, Ukraine, and the United States.

2. Let's Get Cooking!

If you have eaten Chinese food, you will know that many of the ingredients are chopped or sliced into small pieces. If you were asked why, you might say that small pieces are easier to eat with chopsticks. That's partly right, but the most important reason has to do with the environment in which the Chinese live.

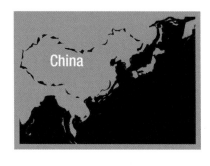

The environment we live in affects what we eat and the way we cook it.

Long ago, in such countries as China, there was very little fuel, such as wood or coal, for making fires.

The Chinese people needed to find a way to cook food quickly, using only a small amount of fuel.

They discovered that food cooks more quickly if it is cut up into smaller pieces. They also developed special cooking pans called woks. Woks have curved sides that allow the heat from a small fire to travel all over the pan, instead of just staying at the bottom.   ⌐ᴊ wok

A wok.

In Japan, there was even less fuel available to use for cooking. The Japanese learned that many foods could be eaten without cooking them. Japanese recipes often use raw fish and vegetables.

Foods that do need to be cooked, such as meat and chicken, are sliced very thinly so that they cook quickly. Because Japan is made up of islands, with little land on which to farm animals, meat is very expensive. Therefore, many Japanese recipes use fish, which is plentiful.

Also, many Japanese foods are eaten with cold, cooked rice. This means that the cook uses only enough fuel to boil rice in one big pot—enough for many meals.

In the hot, dry countries in Mediterranean Europe, North Africa, and the Middle East, people used foods made from plants that had adapted well to the harsh environment. Olives and olive oil came from these areas.

Do You Like Your Olives Green or Black?

Green olives are picked from olive trees before they are fully ripe. Black olives are picked later when they are fully ripe. Olives straight from the tree are too bitter to eat, so they must first be soaked in salty water and other chemicals to take away their bitter taste. Olives contain a nutritious oil that people use for cooking, preserving, and flavoring food.

In extremely cold Arctic areas, where precious fuel was needed for heating, people dried meat and fish to preserve them.

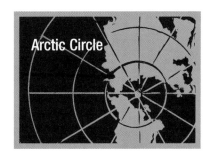

The Arctic is the area of land, sea, and ice near the North Pole. It is home to caribou, polar bears, seals, whales, and many fish.

In New Zealand, some Maori people were lucky enough to live beside hot springs. These are pools of water heated to the boiling point by energy from deep within the earth's crust. To cook, they simply placed meat or vegetables in a flax bag and dropped it into the pool of hot water. Talk about fast food!

3. Don't Forget To Pack Your Taste Buds!

As you have learned, the pasta, potatoes, and turkey we love to eat are not from the cultures and countries we might have guessed.

For hundreds of years, people have been tasting foods from different cultures and returning to their own countries with foods that they think will be popular and easy to grow.

About 700 years ago, an explorer named Marco Polo traveled from Italy to China.

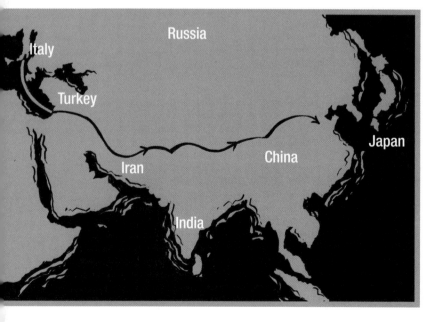

Marco Polo's journey from Italy to China.

Marco Polo was the first European to travel so far from Europe. He returned with some interesting foods and spices that no one in Europe had ever seen or tasted before. One of those foods was pasta!

People in Italy thought that pasta was great to eat. They were able to make it with the wheat that grew in Italy. Eventually, they invented so many different pasta recipes that now most people think the Italians invented pasta.

Making Pasta
Plain pasta is made by mixing wheat flour with water. Colored pasta is made by adding tomatoes, spinach, or other vegetables to the flour and water.

Five hundred years ago, no one in Europe had ever seen a potato. When Spanish soldiers and priests traveled to South America and Mexico, they found many new foods that the people in those places used all the time. The potato was one of them.

Some other foods that the Spanish brought back to Europe were corn, pumpkins, peanuts, tomatoes, peppers, and turkeys! Their meals must have been a lot tastier after that!

Did you know that potatoes and tomatoes come from the same plant family?

The Spanish also brought vanilla beans and cocoa beans (which are used to make chocolate) back from South America. All ice-cream and chocolate lovers must be very grateful for those discoveries!

Chocolate

The word *chocolate* comes from the Aztec word *xocolatl.* "Chocolate" is a lot easier to say! The Aztecs were people who lived in and around Mexico 600 years ago. Most of the world's chocolate is now made from cocoa beans grown in Africa.

Peanuts

Peanuts, which are related to pea plants, originally came from South America. They are unusual because their seed pods push themselves underground to ripen. For this reason, peanuts are sometimes called "ground nuts."

This photograph shows the seed pods. Inside each seed pod are two peanuts.

4. No Time To Cook?

Today we are able to taste foods from many different cultures without leaving our country. Our knowledge of how to grow, store, and transport fresh foods around the world has improved since those times when people could eat only what they could grow and cook themselves from their own environments.

Our knowledge of different cooking methods has also increased as we have learned how different cultures prepare and cook their food.

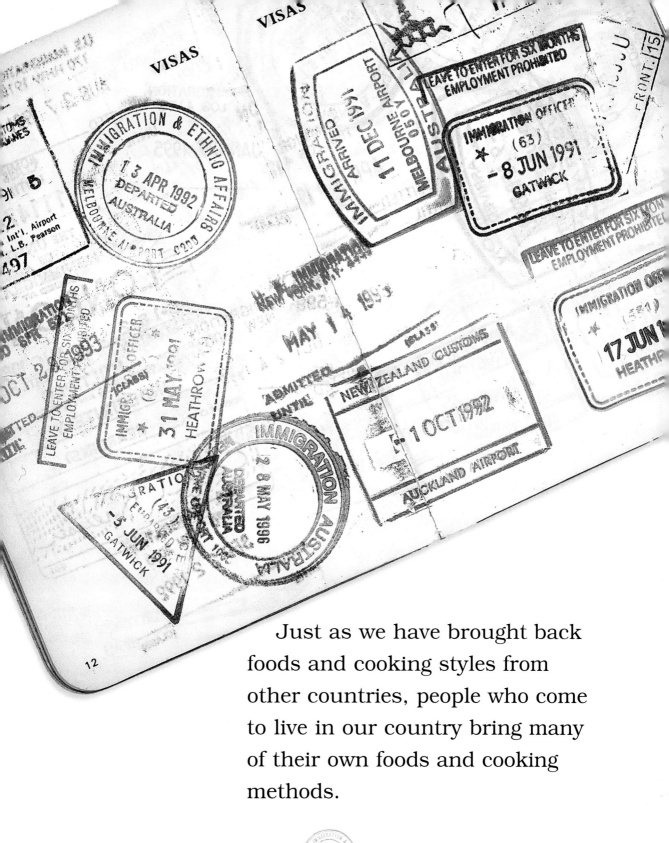

Just as we have brought back foods and cooking styles from other countries, people who come to live in our country bring many of their own foods and cooking methods.

In supermarkets and grocery stores, we can buy food from Europe, Asia, South America, the Pacific Islands, Africa, and the Middle East.

But while we have plenty of fuel for cooking and plenty of foods to cook, there's one thing that many busy people don't have enough of—time!

That's why eating out at restaurants and ordering fast food is so popular. When we need some food in a hurry, we can choose a quick, nutritious meal from a variety of cultures!

23

What's even more fun is that we can take an imaginary trip around the world when we choose to eat out. How about visiting Thailand for some noodles? Or Japan for some sushi? Or England for fish and chips? Or France for crepes? Or Italy for some pasta? Or Greece for a souvlaki? Or Africa for a bean casserole? Or maybe you just feel like a hamburger?

Sometimes fast foods contain a lot of fat, which can make people unhealthy. But some fast foods can also be nutritious. Look for ones that use fresh vegetables, rice, eggs, bread, seafood, and meat. Avoid those that include artificial ingredients and additives. Also, choose foods that are baked, grilled, or cooked in very little oil—they're the most nutritious and very tasty!

A World Of Food

Souvlaki (Greece)

Hamburger (America)

Fish And Chips
(UK, Australia and
New Zealand)

Crepes (France)

Pasta (Italy)

Noodles (Thailand)

Bean Casserole (Africa)

Sushi (Japan)

5. Bon Appetit!

Search the phone book directory and you'll find that foods from many countries are available in your area. What's even better is that you probably already have many of the ingredients they use—you may be able to make the recipes from these restaurants in your own kitchen.

With more and more people traveling around the world and learning about recipes from different cultures, the food you eat no longer depends on where you live and what your environment is like.

There are some things, though, that never seem to become popular outside their home countries. In some parts of Burma, in Asia, a very special meal is made from tea leaves cooked with garlic and crunchy grasshoppers!

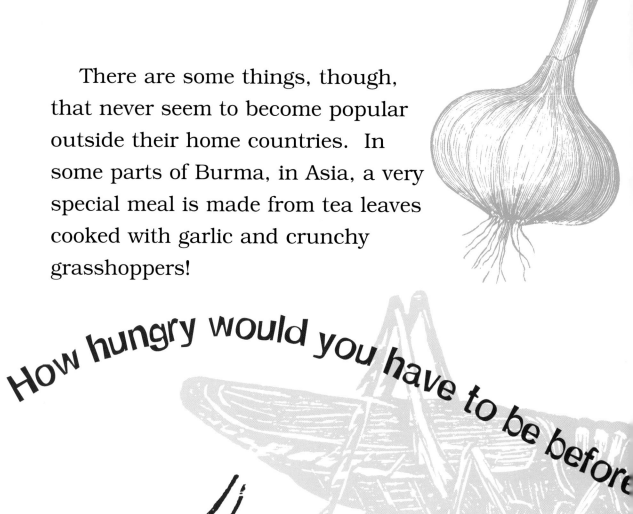

How hungry would you have to be before

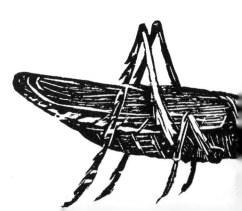

Other Insects On The Menu

Cochineal is a red dye that is often used to color foods like candies and cakes. Cochineal comes from a cactus-eating Mexican insect!

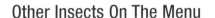

you tried that?

Some people in Australia and New Zealand like to eat the larvae, or young, of some insects. In Australia, witchety grubs are eaten raw from the ground. In New Zealand, a similar larva called a huhu grub is eaten.

Index

Taste Bud Travels

More Bookweb books about foods:

Checkout!—Nonfiction

Inspector Grub

And The Gourmet Mystery—Fiction

The Night Crossing—Fiction

And here's a Bookweb book about how a food allergy makes some ballet dancers very ill:

Understudies—Fiction

Key To Bookweb
Fact Boxes

☐ **Arts**

☐ Health

☐ **Science**

☐ Social Studies

☐ Technology